For the Plot

Hailey Green

BookLeaf Publishing

India | USA | UK

Presentation by *BookLeaf Publishing*

Web: www.bookleafpub.com

E-mail: info@bookleafpub.com

ISBN: 9789358316742

First edition 2023

PREFACE

I once wrote a headline for my life: We live once, we die once, everything in between is irrelevant and for the plot.
But then I shortened it to: lmao yolo :)

Nobody.

Sometimes, I wish you stayed as nobody,
Not just a stranger; a nobody,
Don't try to defend yourself, convince me you're
changing, your image is already set to ruins in
my mind, and there is no saving you,
There is only hate,
Hate for every second of my life you wasted,
every day I spent giving you every piece of my
heart,
To this day, I don't have all of it's shards back, I
know you threw most of them out, even before
things were done, you used them as a cast to
mend your broken heart and when you were all
better you lost them somewhere in the plains we
traveled, the plains you left me in,
No message.
No call.
No love, because this wasn't love,
But how can I say that? When I don't even know
what love is anymore. The only way I found it
was through pockets of gold stolen from second
hand stores, joy of everybody except for myself,
Through the screen of my computer of every
love story I died to live,

Watching through tears as I begged the universe to give me somebody like this to love, I would treat them like they were a human, like they were my choice not some option, I would build them a future with broken fingers and splinter filled skin just so they could take a peek at the happiness I would create for them,
Not for you,
Never, for you.
But it feels like I can't do that anymore, because you wrecked every future I built told me every fault line and watched it crumble, and then you walked away,
You always walked away from me,
Too dysphoric, too depressed, too much self hatred, too much masculinity, too much responsibility to love a liability like me,
Of course, you couldn't love me.
But only I could love you.
I want you to understand everything I did for you.
I need you to feel every second my heart dropped, my tears burnt, my nails scratched beneath layers of skin,
You have to relive all of the moments you failed your promises without a 'thank you' and hurt me without an 'I'm sorry'.
Well are you sorry? No. Of course you're not.

So you'll live in these pages, read the lines I
wrote so you may forever be immortalized in my
pain like a blood-sucking mosquito in amber.
And maybe one day I'll get an apology for you
taking my ability to love,
Or maybe I'll heal and forget every way we
touched,
But I'm not an optimist.

Change?

I think at this point in time, I've learned I can't change.
Give me every reason to, give me pain and suffrage, burn my hands and drown out my shrieks, or even allow me happiness and a world healing of all the sins I buried myself within, I won't change.
I am incapable.
I can't learn what is best for myself because delusion leads me blindly through a field of thorns and convinces me that they are nothing but flowers, I willingly put on the blindfold and tell myself it is all for the best,
Don't tell me it's possible, I've been telling myself that for so long,
Every year it's a new year, but where the hell is the new me?
I'm still a child. Teen. Pitiful. Young. Naive. I've heard all of it before, and I've learned I am nothing more than a shallow person,
I need to be the best, I can't handle criticism, I have to be heard and I need to be acknowledged for all my small deeds or else why the hell did I do them, I have to be loved unconditionally, I can't change my body no matter how many times

I renew my gym membership because I will go
for a few days and then not for weeks, I try to
eat healthy but I tell myself I don't have the time,
I try to be a better person, but it always feels like
I get fucked over.
So no, I can't fucking change.
As badly as I want to.
As much as I want to be anybody more worthy
than myself,
I take self care showers, do my acne routine just
long enough to see a difference, I workout until
everything hurts, I work far more than I sleep, I
delete social media and start to think positively, I
tell myself it's ok to fail, I go for bike rides or
get some sunlight, I read, I start to eat healthier
or even just less, I vent all my negative emotions
and try to see the good around me,
But I fall back into old habits,
Sleep too much, stare at my phone for hours, sob
relentlessly when I mess up, allow my hair to be
slick with grease, I fall into a hole,
Sometimes I willingly crawl back into it because
it feels like home,
There's an inexplainable feeling of nostalgia
being a mess nobody can clean up because
pouring all this effort into myself is mentally
exhausting,
And how could it be worth it?
How could I ever be worth it?

I'm a young, dumb, lacking teen,
I have no faith in myself, I can work 15 hour
days but not spare the time to work on myself,
So how can I change?
I can't.

Shape Shifter

Sometimes I wish I was a shape shifter,
I could be anybody I ever wanted to be, find a
new identity that fits my soul just a little bit
more than the last,
Keep up with the beauty standards, always be
seen as pretty in my own eyes, be able to love
myself if I could,
Each day I could change my hair, eyes, skin,
height, every flaw about myself could be shaped
to perfection in the blink of an eye,
But then who would I be?
Would I still want to be a writer?
Or maybe I'd have the confidence to be a model,
or actress, something requires beauty I know I
am not, the same beauty I erase in the mirror,
redraw my lines so I can be curvier where it
matters, brighter eyes, get rid of my eyebags,
make my face less round,
I'll change myself, slim my body down, but
would I still be myself?
It's important to know that on my journey to self
love, I've always been stumbling over rocky
roads and faced to look at myself growing up,
but never growing old,

If I could be a shapeshifter, I'd stay young, I'd
stay driven, energetic,
In my eyes, if I could change, that means I could
find myself, whoever that is,
The shy reader I dreamt to be as a kid, wearing
sweaters and headphones, round glasses and a
soft face, a friendly, kind woman, pretty in a
weird way and in love with the way the world
breathed around her; but I am not kind.
I wanted to be an extrovert with piercings and
tattoos, a messy abomination to reflect my own
mind and an escape of my own childhood, I'd
dye my hair, be in and out of relationships, turn
into my own shadow; but I am not bold.
Or maybe I'll be a modern housewife, working
from home and going to the work christmas
parties, living an above average life where
nothing is memorable, but I'm at the bare
minimum of happiness; but I want to live.
Ultimately I'm not a shapeshifter,
I am nobody but myself where the only thing I
can change, is my future.
So who will I be?
I've been trying to answer that question for so
long.
I think I'll be myself.
Yeah.
That sounds good.

Super Power

The world won't change unless you make it.
I mean look around, see where we are who we
are,
The lines between good and bad have been
blended and smeared left us colorblind in a
world where everybody thinks differently,
Don't get me wrong, there's nothing bad about
being different only if that difference threatens
the lives of others,
But in my eyes there is no way of saving us with
laws and government,
Those without voices stay without voices while
those who can speak speak over each other and
those with power stay in power,
Even gunshots on the streets, hundreds killed
and hands joined in fear not harmony we are not
listened to,
That's why heroes are overrated, I know, big
jump of reality to hope, but every day is the
same old story,
Headline school shooting, war in Ukraine, Roe
V Wade controlled by white men, but where is
the section of struggling families, suicidal teens,
watered out sparks and a world on fire,
There isn't,

There is no voice,
Because no voice can be heard over gunshots,
over screams of mercy, over the millions of lives
who are treated like cattle, told to play nice and
expected to live a dead American dream,
It seems that voices are not as influential as
money, as titles and pride,
So if I had powers,
Talking comes last as it has always in the past,
Take control of the world and give it a reason to
change, an ultimatum of a better life, a common
threat so everyone will shut up and listen. Truly.
Listen.
Even if it means being a villain, I don't care,
Call me a bad guy, tell me to conform, settle
down, follow the laws, suppress your abilities
because it is your responsibility,
No!
It was the laws responsibility to keep us safe, to
listen, to create the American dream, but this is
nothing but a nightmare!
Power is power,
Don't tell me to not use it if it means that I could
prevent more people suffering,
Don't tell me to be a hero when it would mean I
could be ashamed of not doing what should've
been done a long time ago,
Hero's help the common good,
Spider-Man stays in his neighborhood,

Batman looks over Gotham,
But Thanos united the world against him.
So maybe I could unite the world against me,
If I could do more than speak and dream to
escape this nightmare.
You won't be thanking God; you'll be thanking
me.

Hoodie

I don't wear that hoodie anymore,
Y'know the expensive one bought from some
silly over priced store in Washington DC,
Though I've worn it into a perfect hoodie of soft
comfort I find myself unable to wear it,
I wore it when we spent 3 hours on call every
day though hundreds of miles apart, I wore it the
day I returned back to our city and fell asleep
next to you on the play ground we met at every
time we got a little lonely,
I wore it to our movie nights,
I wore it for us,

The reason I can't wear it isn't because there is
no us anymore,
But because you decided to be a silly goose and
try to commit suicide while wearing it,
Yeah.
In our hoodie.

So now it sits on the back of my door,
Perhaps wondering what it did, why I don't love
it so much anymore,
How one night can ruin a perfectly good
expensive hoodie,

Some times I feel like I could be that hoodie,
Worn and torn from years of usage,
I am not expensive to wear, no, I am a free meal
and gift for anyone who tells me I am anything
more than what I am,

Truth is one night can ruin everything,
Don't tell me I'm wrong,
You can't sit there and shake your head,
Take my heart into your hands trust me, you will
suffer as I did at 6am on a Thursday morning of
late March and a late 'I love you'
I think that was the last time you meant it or the
last time I believed it,

I want to stop writing about you,
I want to move on because I'm happy with who I
am now and I haven't been this healthy in all of
my life,
I have success, I have happiness, I have love,
But I can't help thinking about how we ended,

I can't stop imagining how it should've ended,

I was two words from a cliff with no bottom,
believe me I don't like heights but you
sometimes wonder what it would be like to fall,
Because maybe I could feel anything, everything
I didn't feel towards you,

I could fear for my life,
I could hope that I could fly,
I could cry out in desperate terror for your last
glance but the question is would you hear me?!

You didn't.

I fell. I fell out of love with someone who was
too focused on not loving themself that they
couldn't even love me,
A person who didn't care about the times I
helped and the times I needed help,
It's one thing to have a bad night,
It's another when you wouldn't talk to me so I
downed a few too many pills,
I can't blame you for anything except for your
ignorant neglect,

And now I neglect that hoodie.
That perfect, expensive hoodie on the back of
my door wondering what it did wrong,
Unknowing that I fear to wear it anymore, not
because it reminds me of that one person,
But because it was ruined in a night.

Hoodie Pt. 2

I saw someone wearing that same expensive
hoodie.
Y'know the one from Washington DC? The
same one that hangs on the back of my door,
collecting dust rather than rips of love,
The same one I wore to remind me of you,
And you wore it to leave me,
So it hangs for crimes it did not commit, it's
punished for things it had no guilt towards,
And I wonder, if that other person's hoodie has
done the same?
If there was ever a day where they didn't love it?
Or if there was a day that they absolutely did?
I hope one day I can wear it without
remembering you and what you did,
Not just to that hoodie, but to me,
To my tear soaked bed. To my broken heart I am
still trying to mend,
But it keeps falling apart. It keeps becoming
undone even though I have every reason to love
again, it feels like it's impossible to do it the
same way,
Because now every time I look at that expensive
hoodie, I think of everything it costed to love
you, every moment in time I gave up for you,

every memory I forgot so you could have the
sunlight in my mind,
I remember every kiss we shared and every
bitter taste your words left in the back of my
throat, I remember every night we touched and
every night I was left to hold myself because
you didn't love me as much as I loved you,
In fact you didn't love me!
You can't tell me you loved me!
You don't deserve to love me!
If you can't love yourself, if you can't love every
piece of me, the good and the bad, then you
don't deserve to love me,
And I know, this is too much coming from a
stupid, expensive hoodie,
And I know it's selfish to say what you did was
selfish,
But you ruined that hoodie,
You ruined me,
And I can never love it the same,
I can never love somebody the same,
I blame you,
Not this hoodie.
Not this perfectly, good hoodie.

Everything starts the way it ends

I can't change
I'm still the same
I'm weak
I'm pathetic
I'm begging for light I don't deserve
I boil over, steam red, I am a shrieking kettle
hissing steam that burns anybody who touches
me,
I selfishly ask for space so no one walks away
with blisters,
I hold grudges,
Don't tell me I can forgive them because they
wronged me so long ago,
Because they hurt me so long ago
They left a scar on me
That's what I remember;
Bleeding.
Begging for forgiveness
Only to be answered by absolute silence,
I am reminded most of when I'm alone,
Of cutting my hands on sharp thorns and being
told to stay quiet,
BE QUIET

I am still that pathetic little weak girl I was so
long ago begging for attention, hoping to forgive
myself,
I know she could've forgive me,
Who I have become.
Because when I get upset I can't help but lash
out, I can't help but want the world to feel my
pain, to bleed and suffer as I do,
How selfish is it to want others to truly
understand how I feel?
How pathetic is it to want others to understand?
Because if they understood;
Maybe I would too.

I miss you

Like

A lot

Like words don't mean
                              anything.....

Like there is no way to even speak
Because what good would it do?
You can't feel the aching hole in my chest

You can't feel my touch,
Hands interlinked, a connection I die for every
night,
Skin to skin.
Heart to heart.
Love to love,

Even through prose and lines,
I'm left sinking in this abyss, reaching for the
stars, knowing you are looking there too,

And I hope I will never miss you again,
because you'll be in my arms,
And I won't fear losing you.

I won't have to miss you.

But I do.

Thrifting

I love getting new clothes, new things, new
styles, just NEW!
I'll try things on, find new outfits, finding
different ways I could be beautiful if I am
beautiful, I could buy happiness,
But, I can't thrift everything.
I can't thrift a new heart,
Don't get me wrong, there's no much wrong with
mine,
It's sharp and broken like shattered glass, blood
slightly stained against the edges from my own
negligence,
There are words carved on the walls to remind
me I am not worth what I wish I was,
Don't trip over the soggy buckets filled over the
brim with my tears every time I'm at my limit
and I let everything out,
But if I could thrift a new heart I'd spend a
fortune on pieces of bandages, one the energy to
fix what's been broken,
Don't tell me money cannot buy love because if
it could buy me a heart I would sell my soul,
Because when I thrift clothes I can fix them.
I can cut and sew, replace the rotten parts and
create something everybody wants,

I'm good at fixing things as long as it's not
myself,
Which is why I could fix a thrifted heart,
No matter the stains, the cut edges or even the
stab wounds that still bleed, I could fix it up and
envy the way it can love,
So then I could replace my own, the one I can't
bring myself to fix,
I can thrift a new heart.
Money could buy love.

But thrifting for a new heart is also called
murder and theft,
So this one will have to do.

Problems.

I wish I had teenage problems.
The typical standards of not knowing which
college to choose,
What to be for Halloween or what to ask for for
Christmas,
I wish my problems stayed as nothing more than
wondering if some person likes me, if I'll pass
this class,
Nothing so specific. Nothing as terrifying.
But the problems I deal with aren't normal for a
teenager.
While some girls are worried about looking
pretty I'm scared about looking the same. The
uncut bangs, long straight, bleach dyed hair,
natural looking make up with crop tops and
sweatpants, fake tans and glorifying bodies,
I'm worried about looking like them.
For a teenager I shouldn't be worrying for my
parents financial needs, I shouldn't be working
myself to the core so I don't end up like them. I
focus on my bank account not accounting for my
happiness, I stay busy because if I'm not then
what the hell am I doing?
Why can't I have normal teenage problems?

It's never what do I wear for prom? Who do I ask out?
It's always, will tonight be the night I find my mother dead in the house.
Will she leave a note? Will I see the signs the morning of? Will I be able to stop her?
It's always, how much pressure will it take for me to break this time? Months spent without crying, panic attacks held back by the sheer will that I can't cry. Now of all times, I have things to do. I can't deal with this.
I have a test I need to get an A on, I have work for the next four days, I need my paycheck to be enough so I feel useful,
I'm sick but I can't skip work, it's not that bad, I'll push off my health for the feeling of doing things I'll get praise on, bend my back until it cracks and I fall under the weight of everything I was told I could carry,
Why can't my problems stay as normal teenager problems?
Instead I'm scrolling through social media, wondering why everybody's life is better than mine?
Alcohol, drugs, hookup culture, the only I'm addicted to is being told that I am a success.
That I actually did something, that I will be somebody,
In the long run of things, I'll scared. Petrified.

What if I never amount to being great? What if I
stay a slightly above average individual? No
talent to show. No awards to be praised for?
What if my life is boring?
What if at the end, I'm not ready to die?
I shouldn't be thinking about these things as a
teenager.
This is not normal.
Why can't I be normal?

Death.

Tell me . . . what is death like?

Will I be immortalized? Or will my name be forgotten the moment my blood goes stale, even before my last breath, will I find myself alone?

In a field. One so full of life, yet absolutely dead. Because the moment we realize how alive we are is the same moment we realize just how doomed we are.

I never got over the thought of dying.

A noose around my neck. Too many pills in my system. Clouds blocking my airways until I can't breathe, suddenly I am on the verge of a panic attack wondering what it'll be like when I die,

And I don't want to die.

I don't want to die.

I don't want to die.

So I've never felt more alive . . .

Crying to myself every night in the hallowed
sheets of my bed, realizing just how much of my
life I've already wasted and knowing I'll never
be able to fix it. No matter what I do, I'll never
live up to the full potential I want,

Maybe that's why I want to be a writer. A poet.
Alive. So at least some kind of piece of me will
live longer than my human body, at least I'll die
with the peace of knowing I left something for
people to remember me by.

Maybe that's why I want to feel alive, rebel as a
teenager, live a life to regret and to remember
because after life . . . what is there?

Because I don't believe there's anything.
No afterlife.
No promise land.
No remnants of who you were or what you did.
Not even you.

There's nothing beyond death; except death.

Tropes

By the typical high school movie tropes I've
seen,
I believe I'm a nerd.
Not befriended by many, wearing her classic
glasses and always upholding good grades,
academically smart and always knowing what to
do,

Which is why I hate tropes.

Which is why I hate people who make
something their entire personality,
Which is why I hate myself sometimes when I
do something so predictable, so coordinated in
this faction I've divided myself into,
Which is why it's so hard for me to break out of
that trope.

I'm 17, and an absolute good two-shoes.
I've never drank myself silly, never visited
cloud-9, never had no control over myself other
than the heart ripping, blood sucking, soul
crushing feeling known as unrequited love,
I've been alone more times than I can count,

Hung high and dry in my best outfit because
friends are hard to make and even harder to
keep.

I'm 17 and fail to fall into any trope.
It's frustrating when there is no trope to count
on,
As much as I hate them, but they've formed
factions in my mind that I follow like a rule
book,
I hate them because I can't read certain books
due to how predictable the characters are,

I hate them because now this poem makes no
sense and I am lost in trying to find a faction to
stuff myself inside of.
But I can't.
And now I'm lost.

Somebody to Love

I've only ever had two partners in my life.
No situation-ships, no hook ups, no friends with
benefits, just love.
Most of it is because I've never had much luck
with love.
And one would think that a teenager with more
love than her heart can hold, surely she could
find somebody to love, right?

I was a hopeless romantic all of middle school
and partially into high school. I would cry over
the same boy night after night and convince
myself I am not worthy of love, and I was right.
Nobody every seemed to love me enough, and I
don't know what I did, what I could change, am I
too clingy? Do I ask too much? Why can't I just
love one person forever?

And I was always told I was too young to think
about marrying someone forever, and I guess in
a sense that they're right,
Because I keep ending up in this hole.

I'm so madly in love and then one day I just feel
nothing and I want to run away, I want to hide
my heart and pretend it's all ok,
Like a flashlight that's gone dark, I bang it
against my hand until it works again because
there shouldn't be anything wrong with it, and
yet it still fades.
Why. Why does it always fade?

My first love was one born out of youth. Friends
for years we played together every day at recess,
Nothing got between us, not even when I had
feelings, until suddenly he took a step back and I
was forced to move on.
He dated my best friend.
Broke up with her.
And asked me out.
On and off I tried to get ahold of him, trying to
re-spark our friendship, but it's not the same.
To this day, he sits in my contact list.

My second love wasn't so easy.
Acquaintances turned to my immediate feelings,
I learned that it was hard to not be friends with
somebody that made your palms sweat every
time you got a little too close,
He was never awkward about me confessing,
this time it was me who ran the opposite
direction, took a step back,

I was scared I was making him uncomfortable,
So I fell into the background,
And my feelings never faded, but I did from his
life. To this day, I don't know if he liked me
back, and sometimes I find myself regretting
that.

My third love was the biggest mistake of my
life.
But the first to be requited.

And now I fall to the fourth love of my life, and
how dearly I wished for it to work out,
And yet I keep messing it up. I keep failing at
loving him even if it's the one thing I desired the
most,
So now I sit here,
Wondering if this night is any different than the
ones I lived so long ago,
Crying over love.

I Wish You

I wish you,
I wish you . . . new love,
Don't get me wrong, such a thing can be a
breath of fresh air or the last sigh of exhaustion,
New love is the thresh hold of a new future at
the cost of leaving the past in the darkness, I
worried you wouldn't be able to do it, so I'm
glad you moved forwards,
But don't get it twisted, I can only imagine what
I must be like to love again after what we went
through,
It's not something I wish to think about or go
back to however it is something I wish to discuss
with the shadow of the person I loved and the
hope that you would return,
So tell me, tell me what this new love is like,
Do you hold his hand? Specifically with your
wrist on the top because any other way feels
weird but even then you think it is too
masculine?
When you first kissed him, did you compare his
lips to my own? Did you have a moment of
laughter as he turned away at last moment,
creating an inside joke that was put on lock
down?

Tell me what you give him.
A shoulder? An open DM? A necklace on his
birthday or perhaps is it some junk food from
down the street because you spent all your
money on a fucking hoodie,
Does he give you more than I?
Who am I kidding that's not even possible!
Who can give you three years of selfless love
that tears you inside and out?! Who can spare
every waking moment they have to worrying if
I'll wake up to you dead?! Who can love every
inch of your body, think about you every
moment of every day?! Who can spend every
last cent they have so maybe you could believe
me when I told you you were pretty?!
Who can memorize every little detail of you to
not compliment?! Who could cry every night
without your condolence, without your words of
affection?! WHO COULD WAIT LIKE A
DOG?!
Who could love you?!
And who got their heart shattered day after day,
night after unanswered text pleading for help to
not be alone?
Who fell into manic episodes? Fell in love with
everything I hated about you? Who saw you as
nothing but a mirror of who I am, of who I
was?!

I could scream every ounce of anger left over in
my heart, the rotten infestation of some kind of
pitiful love you never gave me because you
didn't want to! Who taught you how to love and
in return got nothing but loose friends who
won't even hear how bad it hurt!
Surely you got the short end of the stick! The
victim complex of being the last one to love the
other in a relationship but how about you look at
the long end for once in your life?!
I sobbed in your arms helplessly, begging for
another reason why I should keep loving you,
why I should keep hurting myself so you may
stay happy for even a little bit longer-- you
would've rather been dead than spend another
day with me!
Do you know how that felt?
Do you know how that old love spoiled me into
a shell of who I was?!
I can't love like I used to. And I blame you. I
will always blame you. And I will always hate
you, Olive. There is no love left for who I
thought I could love, for someone who couldn't
fucking love me back in every way I begged for.

Perfect Family

Something I'll never have,
I guess I should've known since the moment my
parents divorced that a family built under the
protection of a gold frame would never be under
my possession,
There would be no family dinner every night,
only staring at a sit com on the tv in silence,
I don't know anyone very well on my moms
side, nobody I would trust with secrets or even
ideas of what to get them for Christmas,
I was closer to my dads side, however I don't
think they wanted to be close with me,
My paternal grandparents were always a state
away, always showing up for my brothers band
concerts but when it came to me own, it would
only be my father who attended,
Holidays were the only time of year I would see
my family, pretend that we were fortunate
enough for a bond, for a word of
encouragement, that someone would be proud to
have me as family,
But then the holidays got fewer and fewer,
My family more distant,
My need for their approvement left to starve
unfaithful and foul,

Soon nobody came to my concerts, soon nobody
asked what I was doing in school, soon the A's
were average a B would shake the house,
I would eat alone day by day,
I stopped moving from house to house, took care
of my mother despite every missed opportunity,
She says I don't have to but see if I don't I'll
lose more family more people who should mean
more to my than blood,
I tried to make amends, ask for forgiveness as a
victim, as the runt of the family,
Instead I got body shamed, I got lonely, I got
forgotten and suddenly these people don't feel
like family they feel like failure,
The first holiday I missed was Easter,
I had to work, on the way there my dad
screamed at me in the car because I wouldn't
play a game with my brother,
I couldn't stop crying that whole day,
Next I was left out on the Fourth of July,
I sat poolside to people having fun a jacket over
my stomach because I had surgery a week before
to remove my gallbladder, a result of the eating
disorder I got the moment my grandma told me
how fat I was,
Next, I missed Thanksgiving, my celiac diet
gone unnoticed as my grandma decided to make
noodles, food with wheat and only offered me
vegetable rice,

I've always hated vegetables, I even told her
week prior to get me just plain white rice,
There was no Turkey, no ham, no dumplings or
mashed potato's, just the one type of food I
couldn't eat,
I remember starving that day, the day I thought I
was supposed to eat,
Then came family events I haven't even invited
to,
My dads birthday dinner, he didn't even ask if I
was available, he told me he thought I worked
and didn't bother,
My family missed my choir events, sat through
honors but they weren't happy for me,
Then came my grandpas passing,
I remember them never giving me any chance to
get a momento from him, instead I took one
from his old dresser drawer, I carry it with me to
this day while my brother got a watch and few
other priceless items,
I felt like I was nothing to them, stuck taking
care of my suicidal mother, as well as school and
a full time job, extracurriculars and honors,
I was starved of more than food, but of family
love,
Soon I stopped being invited to Colorado, and
even if I asked to go, I knew it would only be
my grandma body shaming me and food I
couldn't even eat,

I would be a burden,
And now here I am, missed more family dinners
than I knew about,
Dreading the day of Thanksgiving because I
know nobody will be giving me any thanks for
keeping my mother alive, for surviving the life
of no love they could provide for me,
All I've ever wanted was for a happy family,
We didn't need to be rich or better off, just
happy,
A family dinner now and then
A notice of everything I've done
But that's too much to ask for,
And besides,
I can't even see them as family anymore.

My Frustrations

Feel more than frustrations, they feel like
weights. Mountains that pressure me into a small
space, and I am no diamond, for I go in as a gem
and come out as a lump of coal,
I didn't charge my chromebook, my earbuds
aren't charged,
My worries are small but they build,
I forgot my energy drink, my boyfriend isn't at
school,
It keeps stacking upwards,
I didn't get into the committee I wanted and I
got booted from the book I wanted to read for
AP Lit,
I'm stressed over an essay I got a 2+ on, one I
can always rewrite but I didn't get it right the
first time so what is the point? I can't improve,
that pressure is building,
I can't get Halloween off because I work at a
fast food joint as a teenager, my manger doesn't
think I deserve a Halloween even though it's my
favorite holiday, not to mention last year my ex
refused to spend the day together and the year
before they were violently ill,

I won't get overtime because this is a shitty job,
I can't dress up, and I'll be working 4-11 so
there's no trick-or-treating.
See everything builds over time because my luck
has disappeared,
I'll have to tutor some person and they'll look at
me like I'm dumb,
When I tell people I am having a bad day I mean
I am one word from strangling the next person
out of absolute despair because I can't make this
day any better,
I am left with this god awful luck and look
what's next? It's a Monday.
I have work tonight to finish off the worst my
luck,
And I hope tomorrow is better. I hope it comes
soon.

Love Attempts

I'd love to say that my first attempts to find love
were as romantic as any eight year old could be,
but I don't think he liked girls who growled at
him like a wolf, or who constantly stalked him at
recess,
It was just mixed signals in my eyes, how was I
supposed to know that I wasn't supposed to bark
at him if I wanted him to like me?
But I want to say I improved, sixth grade I liked
someone in my gym class, like anybody else I
stalked him to his locker and took a picture, now
I know what you're saying-- why didn't I learn
to not stalk someone the first time it didn't work
out?
Because if it doesn't work the first time it's
obviously just because they didn't like me so I
need to try it again a second time, and a third
time, and now it's been five attempts? I'm
starting to realize I might be doing something
wrong,
I still have this kid's picture on my old phone
too, not in a creepy way but as a way to
normalize that things I did wrong as a kid and
evidence that my parents didn't love me enough,

And in the process of my 'normalized' stalking,
I also managed to gaslight myself that he liked
me back, when in fact it was his friend who
liked me, awkward
So I moved on, not by deleting his picture and
calling it good but by finding a new obsession, a
new victim-- I mean boy,
And he was cute, and blond, and blue eyes
meaning we're related by some kind of long
blood line but we're normalizing that and he
totally liked me back, that's not just me being
crazy, I know all of the movie tropes and he
looked at me for exactly 1.39 seconds, and not to
flex or anything, he was looking right at me as I
took of a photo of him,
Which by the way, he's always photogenic, even
if not by his own knowledge.
But oh how the tables can turn when someone
asks me out, which nowadays is asking someone
for their insta or snap, which I only have one of
the two,
So I was working at my old job which was a fast
food cashier on a slow Saturday, I'd been clean
from obsession for maybe 13 hours, but
anyways this kid comes up to ask for a to-go
box,
I give him one and he asks if he can get my
TikTok,
TikTok?

A for effort but I would've taken a photo and
came back every Saturday at the same time just
to gaslight myself into thinking that when I get
asked if I was any sauce I think I'm being flirted
with,
Sure I may be delusional, but hey, at least I
believe I can pull anybody I want,
And look at me now, with my boyfriend of ten
months who I do not growl at, maybe because I
know that it's not-- in fact-- the way to get
someone to like you, or maybe it's because he
used to bully kids like me in elementary school.

Him

He reminds me of home,
Though he isn't composed of four walls and a
roof that leaks occasionally into boxes placed
down in the kitchen, his arms put me into a safe
where nobody could ever hurt me as much as his
sad brown eyes,
I can't say I've ever enjoyed homes, kerosene
seems to paint every image of a house in my
mind,
The slightest spark setting the whole thing
ablaze and well-- in a matter of seconds there
was no home, only a pile of ashe slipping
between my fingers,
Which is why I love the way his fingers merely
interlace through mine, there is no slipping, no
holding on for dear life,
He reminds me of winter's laugh,
The feeling of bitter cold knocking at my bones
and whispering against my cheeks, don't get me
wrong I hate the winter, but there's something
just so nostalgic about this love, I can't see
myself ever walking away willingly,
The way his silhouette fills every dream I had as
a little girl waiting for love,
I've always been in love with the feeling of love,

I've always been in love with the version of
myself where love was more than a possibility,
So in any case I'd say I've always been in love
with this boy,
Or at least, I was in love with the way we met
early in my middle school years, the beginning
of my hopeless romantic emotions and the way I
watched him in art,
I couldn't help but wonder if anybody saw past
the painting and sculptures van gough made, just
to examine him himself and see him as the true
piece of art,
Which is why any time I go into an art class, it
reminds me of him,
And I imagine his hands powdered with dry
clay, dressed in a white t-shirt and a stained
apron hugging loose around his waist, I can't
help but imagine his smile,
Yes that smile he bore the first time I really
looked at him as he ran to a table to steal paint,
The same smile he wore when he walked right
back into my life,
He reminds me of any kind of old dusty book I
would find in a library,
The kind of book where the cream colored pages
brush against your fingers and leave a
remarkable scent you could never find anywhere
else, the kind of book that you could never put

down because of how indulged you are within
it's pages,
Captured straight from my imagination he
reminds me of every night I cried over finding
love, healing any wound that still bleeds inside
of my soul,

Typical Teen Girls... I Guess

Rage
If you know any female characters in any show
ever you know if the not-so-rare sight of her
losing her temper,
If you have a sibling or friend with a spit fire
tongue you can maybe understand the shock of
what words spill from their mouth in a fit of
overwhelming emotion that boils in their gut
raising the heat in their cheeks until they YELL!
I wasn't always an angry person,
A bomb lit from both ends and once the spark is
lit nothing can stop it from counting down the
weeks, days, hours, seconds that it will explode
in a ball of flame and hurt feelings,
Maybe I inherited my temper from my dad,
A man who spoke of no emotion until a simmer
turned to a red hot boil, spilling over the pot and
sizzling upon the stove until you are suffocating
in tears of mercy from his poisonous bite,
I didn't understand but when I started to grow up
I found just where my fuse was,
December twenty second I went to work without
my hat, I had to call my dad to grab my hat and
when he did he yelled at me for being stubborn,
So the scene is set,

A teenage girl in her fitted work outfit in fast
food customer service, a tongue still too dull to
spit anything back but her cheeks flushed with
red hornets and too much on her mind to even
see straight,
Her fuse lit brighter than the sun, her gut twisted
and wrenched in the anger that made it all too
difficult to just stand there,
She would take the christmas ornament she
made on the tree by the entrance, crush it
between her fingers and let the blood gush to the
ground, at least then she could feel anything but
this suffocating rage stuck inside of her gut
clawing for freedom,
Her hat thrown to the ground and her skin frozen
as she steps out into the bitter wind of the
outdoors so that maybe she can cool off, so
maybe she doesn't have to YELL!
But instead she cries. And the tears fizzle out the
fuse.
Now the fuse is water resistance, it's hazardous
presence always right there at the tip of her
tongue and tying a noose around her tolerance,
She built up for moments like this, trained
herself to breathe and shut down so that fuse
never got lit, never got messed with because the
slightest thing could create an impairable hole
within her life,

But it builds up again, It's always still building
up,
Suddenly I'm being forced back into what I
avoided with my childhood, the rules, the eating,
the loss of freedom, the dependency that could
be cured with trust,
Blow out the fuse! Fire in the hole here it all is
again, buried underneath a grave of gunpowder
and triggering subjects,
Tell me to eat less and now I can't eat at all, I
healed and mended but now I am reminded of
every meal I skipped, every ping of hunger in
my stomach that gave me more pride than any
unspoken good job I received from my parents,
Anger at the failure I have become because I am
a naive little girl in the world of wolves I don't
have the morals of biting back until my teeth
grow in,
Every little thing is eating at me,
Something doesn't load,
I can't see the light of day,
I can't eat
I can't sleep
I can't work
I can't write
I can't stop this fuse from starting on fire,
I can't cry
I can't shut down,
I can't breathe,

I can't stop digging my early grave
I can't even scream for my own sanity,
I am going to implode with this rage!
I am going to YELL!
But nothing I do will make me feel better.

Eulogy, No Not Really You Bitch.

Let's try this again,
One last, final time before I am laid to rest, my
sins written across my body, I stopped caring to
read them because I stopped caring about my
life,
Somewhere along the way to this ending I
became reckless, deceitful, full of so much hate
that it started to rot my corpse out hollow
because what else am I supposed to do?
I've changed,
And I don't know if it was for the better,
I can tell myself that it was intentional, that my
skin thickened and my glass half full turned half
empty whenever I look at someone and only see
the things I could possibly hate about them,
Did I do this on purpose?
I adapted to my situationship, I turned myself
inside out so that I could wash myself off and
clean off my eyes so I could see clearly,
Tell me why all I can see in this world is hate?!
Vile and cruel while I wished all I could do was
love, but let me tell you I do not have the heart
strings left to be played for years, left on the lit
up end of a phone, kept on my toes for a text, a

message, a notification, any sign of life that
mine was loved like it should,
Tell me how long you planned on leaving me
waiting?! Show me all the tears you've shed so I
can feel like I meant something,
Tell me what I can do to remove your curse over
me?!
I told you everything I was scared of, you took
my home and placed it under siege, you told me
to come running home to a locked door I
would've spent eternity knocking down if I
knew it would benefit me in any way, any shape,
any form you wish for me to take on so I could
hold you better, closer,
You took my innocence, my love, you made me
less of who I was and when I called it quits you
left me back in the gutter I saved you from,
Tell me how you give me my life back? My love
back? My persistence and heart worth holding
on the cold rainy nights, tell me how-- how am I
supposed to live?
Because I'm tired of living in the casket of who
I was. I'm tired of reaching into the hole in my
chest to find an ounce of love so I can pretend to
be the same romantic I once was,
You left me in a hole I see no way of climbing
out of, seeking the darkness for kind eyes when
all I can find are blades that scratch my flesh in
every way your words did,

You told me I wasn't worth it, you told me you
loved me and all I could do was cry at just how
empty those words were to me, you left me in
the lowest pits of my sanity and told me to get
high on the fumes of burning memories,
No pictures, no touching anywhere below the
neck, no dancing, no dates, no flowers, over two
years and not a singular flower?! No Valentine's,
no expensive gifts, no free gifts, no joy riding,
no swimming, no friends who don't understand
every detail of your struggles, I guess I was one
of those friends, the friends you left behind
because I didn't understand?!
You left me behind, because my love didn't
outweigh your self-hate,
How am I supposed to heal when you left me so
much grief? So much wasted time? How could I
have ever loved somebody who never once
loved me?
I've changed, I think we both have.

Flying

What is it like to fly?
Well, it's quite beautiful,
It's the cool rush of wind praising every inch of
your skin with a motherly touch many have
forgotten,
It's the delicacy of a floating lily pad pushing
across the ripples of a turquoise pond reflecting
tangerine skies,
Flying was so much more than the sights of
rosette petals and copper leaves,
It was a dopamine high that took off every sad
piece of your mind and scooped your hands
within it's own,
It put you in a field of golden wheat and sung a
lullaby that lured you into the sky,
And following the sweet melody was too
irresistible to withstand with a heart praising a
harmony unheard,
So the feeling of flying is stripped of a social
bubble and filled instead with a love for your
harmony's notes,
It's flaws of perfection and calming sensation
that pour molten gold into your shoes,
You're flying,
You're free,

You're falling.

Those romantic cherry blossoms turn into
droplets of blood that warm your skin,
Your wings tear to the bone detaching
themselves with a rejected hatred,
You're left falling into an unpromised demise
where only frost touches your skin and leaves
blackened patches of pain,
Fall further until your harmony cracks with the
denial tears,
Chase away your frost bitten fears with those
crimson wings, see flying is everything but easy,
It's beauty and pain intermingled after a tango
gone wrong,
And it's a heartless fear that's followed by
everything but a sweet success,
So what is it like to fly?
I have no idea,
Because the only thing I remember is the fall.